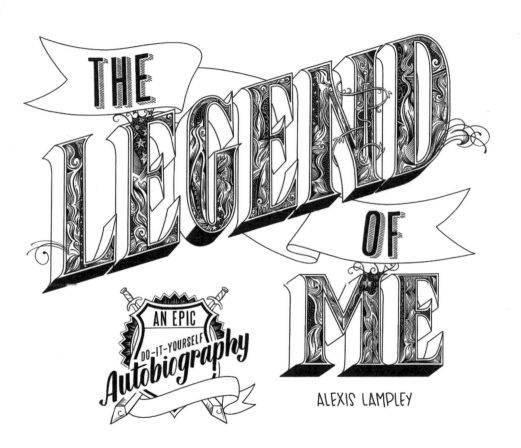

THE LEGEND OF ME

AN EPIC DO-IT-YOURSELF Autobiography

OF ME

ALEXIS LAMPLEY

ROCK POINT

Brimming with creative inspiration, how-to projects, and useful information to enrich your everyday life, Quarto Knows is a favorite destination for those pursuing their interests and passions. Visit our site and dig deeper with our books into your area of interest: Quarto Creates, Quarto Cooks, Quarto Homes, Quarto Lives, Quarto Drives, Quarto Explores, Quarto Gifts, or Quarto Kids.

TO THOSE WHO SEE MAGIC IN
THE ORDINARY - AND TO THOSE
WHO MAKE IT. NEVER STOP.

CONTENTS

WELCOME TO MY Legend

THIS IS THE RECORD OF A BRAVE ___ HERO, AN EPIC TALE OF THE LIFE—AND THE LEGEND—OF ME. LIFE IS AS MUCH AN ADVENTURE AS WE MAKE IT, AND I'M MAKING THE MOST OF MINE. DOCUMENTED WITHIN THIS BOOK IS THE EXTRAORDINARY QUEST OF MY EVERYDAY LIFE AND THE EPICNESS THAT IS ME: _____

CHARACTER PROFILE

BEFORE I EMBARK ON THIS JOURNEY, I MUST DISCOVER WHAT I'M MADE OF. AS I TRAVERSE THESE PAGES, MY CHARACTER ATTRIBUTES AND BASIC CHARACTERISTICS -BOTH ESSENTIAL ASPECTS OF WHO I AM- WILL HAVE BEARING ON MY SUCCESS (OR BE FOREMOST IN MY UNDOING).

PRIMARY CHARACTERISTICS

RUMORS ARE THAT I'M TEN FEET TALL AND SHOOT LASERS FROM MY EYES, BUT NOT ALL RUMORS ARE TRUE.

HEIGHT

HAIR COLOR

EYE COLOR

GENDER

BLOOD TYPE
(A-NEGATIVE, Z-POSITIVE, RADIOACTIVE, DELICIOUS, ETC.)

IDENTIFYING MARKS

DATE OF BIRTH

UNCOMMON PHYSICAL CHARACTERISTICS

BODY TYPE

DEXTERITY
(RIGHT-HANDED, LEFT-HANDED, AMBIDEXTROUS)

SPECIES
(HUMAN, ELF, CYBORG, ETC.)

NAME

SKIN COLOR
(BROWN, BLUE, IVORY, SPOTTED, IRIDESCENT, ETC.)

ALIASES

STAR SIGN

MY AVATAR

A VISUAL REPRESENTATION OF MYSELF, REALISTIC OR OTHERWISE

CHARACTER

BARBARIAN

STRONG
SIMPLE
RESILIENT
LOUD

A WARRIOR WHO RELIES ON BRUTE STRENGTH.

Bard

CHARISMATIC
MUSICAL
CREATIVE
FUN

AN ARTIST WHOSE GIFT INSPIRES
THOSE AROUND ME.

Archivist

BRILLIANT
BOOK-SMART
HARD-WORKING
NERDY

A KEEPER OF KNOWLEDGE AND STUDIER
OF THE PAST.

NOBLE

PROPER
SINGLE-MINDED
PRINCIPAL-ORIENTED
ELEGANT

A CLASSY RULE-MAKER WITH A PENCHANT
FOR POLITICS.

RANGER

PRAGMATIC
WOODSY
SELF-SUFFICIENT
ALOOF

A HUNTER AND TRACKER LIVING OFF THE LAND.

Sorcerer

POWER-HUNGRY
AMBITIOUS
FEARLESS
VOLATILE

A WARLOCK USING RAW MAGICAL TALENT TO GET AHEAD.

CLASS

MY IDENTITY MOST CLOSELY ALIGNS WITH:

Wizard

MAGICAL
STRANGE
DOMINATING
EXTRAORDINARY

A MAGE USING SPELLS AND WISDOM TO SHAPE MY WORLD.

CLERIC

LOYAL
RULE-ORIENTED
UNFLAPPABLE
FAITHFUL

A HEALER/NURTURER WHOSE FAITH DRIVES ME.

ROGUE

CUNNING
STREET-SMART
ATTRACTIVE
REBELLIOUS

A THIEF/PIRATE RELYING ON STEALTH AND WIT.

PALADIN

DUTIFUL
PROTECTIVE
TENACIOUS
UNSTOPPABLE

A CRUSADER FIGHTING FOR TRUTH AND JUSTICE.

SMITH

HANDS-ON
ARTISTIC
FOCUSED
TOUGH

A MAKER WHOSE HARD WORK BREEDS RESULTS.

VILLAIN

PITILESS
SELF-CENTERED
RESOURCEFUL
HONEST

A RUTHLESS RULE-BREAKER WITH A SINGULAR GOAL.

Attributes

1-6   I'M BELOW AVERAGE
6-11   I'M AVERAGE
12-15   I'M ABOVE AVERAGE
16-19   I'M A PRODIGY
20-23   I'M SUPERHUMAN

MY CHARACTER ATTRIBUTES ARE RATED ON A SCALE OF 1-23. I'M RATING MYSELF ON THIS SCALE IN EACH CATEGORY TO BETTER ILLUMINATE MY CHARACTER AND EQUIP MYSELF DURING MY QUEST.

STRENGTH

1 ├─┼─┤ 2

MY STRENGTH IS DETERMINED IN PART BY MY CHARACTER CLASS. HERE IS AN ACCOUNT OF MY PHYSICALITY AND DEXTERITY AND THE WAY THEY APPLY TO THE WORLD I LIVE IN.

MY EXCEPTIONAL PHYSICAL ABILITIES INCLUDE:

....

....

MY PHYSICAL LIMITATIONS/CHALLENGES ARE:

....

....

MY STRENGTH LIES IN MY .... MUSCLE(S).

WHAT STRENGTH LOOKS LIKE TO ME:

I CONSIDER MY ACTIVITY LEVEL TO BE:

☐ I'M A MACHINE
☐ HYPERACTIVE
☐ REGULARLY ACTIVE
☐ MODERATE
☐ LEVEL ZERO

TO PREPARE MYSELF FOR BATTLE, I CHOOSE TO TRAIN BY:

☐ RUNNING ☐ WALKING
☐ HIKING ☐ BIKING
☐ DANCING ☐ SWIMMING
☐ OTHER ....

MY WEAPON OF CHOICE IS:

☐ AXE ☐ BOW & ARROW
☐ KNIFE ☐ SWORD
☐ MY HANDS ☐ THROWING STA
☐ POISON ☐ STAFF
☐ WAND ☐ SHIELD
☐ OTHER ....

IN GENERAL MY AIM IS:

PASSING   GOOD   AWESOME

ABYSMAL ├────────────────────────────┤ PROFESSIONAL

DECENT   GREAT

THE ADVENTURE I SEEK WOULD BE MOST LIKE:

☐ WALKING ACROSS VAST, DANGEROUS LANDS TOWARD UTTER DOOM, WITH FRIENDS.
☐ TRAVELING CROSS COUNTRY, HUNTING MONSTERS WITH FAMILY.
☐ DEFENDING MYSELF AND MY HOME AGAINST HOARDES OF UNDEAD.
☐ USING MY POWERS TO DEFEND MANKIND AND UPHOLD PEACE.
☐ MAKING DO WITH MY CREW, TAKING ANY JOB THAT PAYS, ROAMING THE UNIVERSE.
☐ LEARNING TO USE MAGIC AT A SECRET SCHOOL.
☐ OTHER ....

Constitution

1 —|—|—|—|—|—|—|—|—|—|—|—|—|—|—|—|—|—|—|—|—|—|— 23

HERE IS AN ACCOUNT OF MY INTERNAL FORTITUDE, SHOWING WHAT I'M MADE OF ON THE INSIDE:

I'M ALLERGIC TO:...

THE WORST ILLNESS I'VE EVER HAD IS:.....................................

HOW I FELT:..

I HAVE SUFFERED.................BROKEN BONES:..........................

I HAVE HAD..REMOVED FROM MY BODY.

I NEED.............HOURS OF SLEEP TO FUNCTION.

THE GREATEST AMOUNT OF PHYSICAL PAIN I'VE EVER ENDURED WAS:..........

....

I AM STRENGTHENED BY:...

I AM DRAINED BY:...

WHEN I USE ALL MY ENERGY, I MUST....................TO RECHARGE.

I CAN HOLD MY BREATH FOR....................SECONDS.

I CAN RESIST BLINKING FOR:..

I HAVE STRONG WILLPOWER WHEN IT COMES TO:............................

....

I HAVE WEAK WILLPOWER WHEN IT COMES TO:..............................

....

WITHOUT SUSTENANCE, I:

- ☐ GET ANGRY
- ☐ AM UNAFFECTED
- ☐ CAN'T THINK
- ☐ OTHER..............
- ☐ BECOME WEAK
- ☐ FEEL STRONGER
- ☐ BECOME DELIRIOUS

I'D HOLD UP UNDER TORTURE UNTIL:

- ☐ EATING A BUG
- ☐ WATERBOARDING
- ☐ OTHER:
- ☐ TICKLING
- ☐ A SONG ON REPEAT
- ☐ SOCIAL INTERACTION

19

INTELLIGENCE

1 ├─┼─┼─┼─┼─┼─┼─┼─┼─┼─┼─┼─┼─┼─┼─┼─┼─┼─┼─┤ 2?

SOME CALL THIS "BOOK-SMARTS." THIS IS HOW I STACK UP.

I HAVE COMPLETED.................YEARS OF EDUCATION
MY SPECIFIC CONCENTRATION OF STUDY:...
I CONSIDER MYSELF A QUICK LEARNER: Y/N
I AM FLUENT IN...............LANGUAGE(S):...
I KNOW ENOUGH OF.............LANGUAGES TO GET BY:.................................
I CAN READ/WRITE/SPEAK.....................FICTIONAL LANGUAGE(S):...............

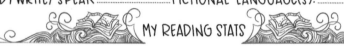 MY READING STATS

AVERAGE WORDS PER MINUTE:

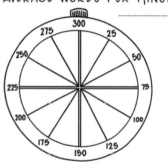

AVERAGE BOOKS PER YEAR:

AVERAGE BOOKS PER WEEK:

AVERAGE BOOKS
PER MONTH:

20

wisdom

1 —|—|—|—|—|—|—|—|—|—|—|—|—|—|—|—|—|—|—|—|—|—|— 23

SOME CALL THIS "STREET-SMARTS". IT SHOWS MY COMMON SENSE AND PERCEPTIONS,
INCLUDING THOSE ABOUT MYSELF.

FEW PEOPLE KNOW I HAVE THIS TALENT:..

IF MY SOUL MANIFESTED AS AN ANIMAL, IT WOULD BE:..........................

OTHERS WOULD DESCRIBE ME AS:...

I WOULD DESCRIBE MYSELF AS:..

IF I HAD NO OBLIGATIONS, I WOULD...ALL DAY.

THE BEST COMPLIMENT I'VE RECEIVED:..

THE WORST INSULT I'VE SUFFERED:...

...I CAN SPIN THAT INTO A POSITIVE BY:..

THINGS I NEVER WANT TO CHANGE ABOUT MYSELF:...................................

....

....

THINGS I WISH I COULD IMPROVE ABOUT MYSELF:.....................................

....

....

THINGS I WOULD LIKE TO BELIEVE ABOUT MYSELF, BUT AREN'T REALLY TRUE:

....

....

....

....

ON A SCALE OF NAIVE CARTOON PRINCESS TO WORLD-WORN ONE-EYED ELDER, I AM:
HEEDLESS ▭▭▭▭▭▭▭▭▭▭▭▭▭▭▭▭▭▭▭ VIGILANT

LUCK

1 ┼┼┼┼┼┼┼┼┼┼┼┼┼┼┼┼┼┼┼┼┼ 23

THERE'S A DASH OF LUCK INVOLVED IN ANY HERO'S JOURNEY. THIS IS HOW CHANCE WILL FACTOR INTO MY QUEST:

FATE IS IN .... HANDS.   I [HAVE / HAVE NEVER] WON SOMETHING

LUCKY THINGS / EXPERIENCES

UNLUCKY THINGS / EXPERIENCES

Attributes Recap

AN EASY REFERENCE GUIDE

STRENGTH

1 ├─┼─┤ 23

Constitution

1 ├─┼─┤ 23

INTELLIGENCE

1 ├─┼─┤ 23

Wisdom

1 ├─┼─┤ 23

LUCK

1 ├─┼─┤ 23

BEST QUALITIES

WORST QUALITIES

Represents Me

IF I WERE A _____ I WOULD BE...

BOOK

FICTIONAL CHARACTER

TV SHOW

MOVIE

GAME

SONG

Affects Me

THIS_____ HAS MOST AFFECTED ME:

BOOK

FICTIONAL CHARACTER

TV SHOW

MOVIE

GAME

SONG

PREFERENCES

WHAT WE LIKE INFLUENCES WHO WE ARE,
AND GIVES US COMMON GROUND ON
WHICH WE CAN CONNECT WITH OTHERS.
HERE ARE THE THINGS THAT HELP DEFINE
MY PATH.

FAVORITES

BOOKS: ....

GENRES: ....

MOVIES: ....

TV SHOWS: ....

PRODUCER: ....

DIRECTOR: ....

MUSIC: ....

LYRICS: ....

BANDS: ....

SINGERS: ....

GAMES: ....

ACTORS: ....

ACTRESSES: ....

WRITERS: ....

ARTISTS: ....

COMEDIANS: ....

WEBSITES: ....

SOCIAL MEDIA: ....

NEWS SOURCE: ....

TIME OF DAY: ....

DAY OF WEEK: ....

HOLIDAY: ....

SEASON: ....

NUMBER: ....

COLOR:
LETTER:
SMELLS:
FOOD:
MEAL:
DRINK:
DESSERT:
RESTAURANT:
FLOWER:
CLOTHES/OUTFIT:
TOYS/GADGETS:
HOBBIES:
PLACE TO RELAX:
CITY:
FICTIONAL CITY:
COUNTRY:
WORLD/PLANET/DIMENSION:
SPORT:
MYTHICAL CREATURE:
ANIMAL:
VILLAIN:
HERO:
SIDEKICK:
SUPERPOWER:
THING TO DO ON A RAINY DAY:
THING TO DO ON A SUNNY DAY:
THING TO COLLECT:
QUOTE:

LIKES

LIKE

DISLIKES

DISLIKE

MORALS

I STAND FOR WHAT IS RIGHT...BUT WHAT IS RIGHT ANYWAY?

I WOULD DO WHAT IS RIGHT INSTEAD OF WHAT IS EASY...
- ☐ NO MATTER THE COST
- ☐ ONLY IF NO ONE GOT HURT BUT ME
- ☐ ONLY IF IT DIDN'T HURT ME

I WOULD MAKE A DEAL WITH THE DEVIL IN RETURN FOR: ....

I WILL NEVER GIVE UP MY HABIT OF: ....

I LIE:
- ☐ RARELY, IF EVER
- ☐ OFTEN
- ☐ TO PROTECT MYSELF
- ☐ BY OMISSION

- ☐ OCCASIONALLY, ABOUT INSIGNIFICANT THINGS
- ☐ ONLY IF THE TRUTH IS UNHELPFUL AND MEAN
- ☐ TO PROTECT SOMEONE ELSE
- ☐ OTHER ....

I [HAVE / HAVE NOT] STOLEN...
THE CIRCUMSTANCES WERE: ....

I [HAVE / HAVE NOT] BEEN ARRESTED...
THE CIRCUMSTANCES WERE: ....

I [HAVE / HAVE NOT] CHEATED...
THE CIRCUMSTANCES WERE: ....

I [HAVE / HAVE NOT] TRESPASSED...
THE CIRCUMSTANCES WERE: ....

IF THERE WERE NO REPERCUSSIONS, I WOULD: ....

I WOULD FIGHT IN A WAR IF: ....

OPINIONS

Y CHOICE:

MORNING · MIDDAY · EVENING · DEAD OF NIGHT

SWEET · SALTY · SAVORY

BREAKFAST · SECOND BREAKFAST · LUNCH · DINNER · DESSERT

TOO HOT · TOO COLD

SILENCE · NOISE

BOOK · MOVIE

MUSIC · LYRICS

MOUNTAINS · OCEAN · DESERT · PLAINS · FOREST

FIRE · WATER · AIR · EARTH · METAL

RAIN · SHINE

FICTION · NON-FICTION

DRAWING · WRITING

ANIMATED · LIVE-ACTION

DIGITAL WORLD · FANTASY WORLD · REAL WORLD

FRUIT · VEGETABLE

WRITTEN · SPOKEN

....IN MODERATION.

....IN ABUNDANCE.

PEOPLE MAKE TOO MUCH OF A BIG DEAL OUT OF:..

....

PEOPLE NEED TO MAKE A BIGGER DEAL ABOUT:...................................

....

ISSUES I'M WILLING TO ARGUE ABOUT:..

....

Beliefs

	SHOULD	SHOULDN'T
CHILDREN		
GOVERNMENT		
PEOPLE		
FAMILIES		
RELIGION		
MEN		
WOMEN		
MOVIES		
TV		
MUSIC		
BOOKS		
GAMES		
SPORTS		
CELEBRITIES		
TEACHERS		
LIFE		
DEATH		

I BELIEVE IN:
☐ EVOLUTION ☐ CREATION ☐ REINCARNATION
☐ NOTHING ☐ OTHER: ....

ASTROLOGY IS: ....

THERE IS POWER IN A NAME / WORD. [TRUE / FALSE]

BELIEVE:

GOALS

Y GOALS ARE

DREAMS and WISHES

Y DREAMS ARE

43

Backstory

THE ONLY FAMILY WE HAVE A SAY IN ARE THE ONES WE CHOOSE FOR OURSELVES. FOR BETTER OR WORSE, THESE ARE THE PEOPLE WHO HELPED SHAPE WHO I AM. SINCE FAMILIES COME IN ALL SHAPES AND SIZES, THIS RECORD IS KEPT IN THE WAY THAT BEST FITS MINE.

A PORTRAIT OF MY YOUNGER SELF

GUARDIANS

NAME: ....
ROLE: ....
COULD BE DESCRIBED AS: ....
REMINDS ME OF THIS PERSON / CHARACTER:

....

WE ARE MOST ALIKE IN THESE WAYS:

....

....

WE ARE DIFFERENT IN THESE WAYS:

....

....

MY FAVORITE THING ABOUT THEM: ....

NAME: ....
ROLE: ....
COULD BE DESCRIBED AS: ....
REMINDS ME OF THIS PERSON / CHARACTER:

....

WE ARE MOST ALIKE IN THESE WAYS:

....

....

WE ARE DIFFERENT IN THESE WAYS:

....

....

MY FAVORITE THING ABOUT THEM: ....

48

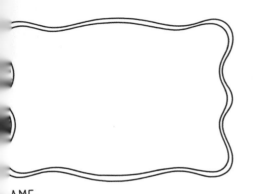

AME: ....
OLE: ....
HE BEST WAY TO DESCRIBE THEM: ....

1Y FAVORITE THING ABOUT THEM: ....
....

NAME: ....
ROLE: ....
THE BEST WAY TO DESCRIBE THEM: ....

MY FAVORITE THING ABOUT THEM: ....
....

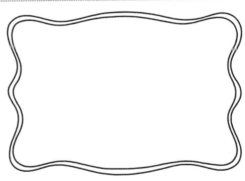

NAME: ....
ROLE: ....
THE BEST WAY TO DESCRIBE THEM: ....

MY FAVORITE THING ABOUT THEM: ....
....

NAME: ....
ROLE: ....
THE BEST WAY TO DESCRIBE THEM: ....

MY FAVORITE THING ABOUT THEM: ....
....

49

Siblings

I HAVE: .... SIBLING(S).

NAME: ....
COULD BE DESCRIBED AS: ....
REMINDS ME OF (PERSON/CHARACTER): ....

WE ARE MOST ALIKE IN THESE WAYS:
....
....

WE ARE DIFFERENT IN THESE WAYS:
....
....

MY FAVORITE THING ABOUT THEM:
....

SISTER / BROTHER / IN-LAW

NAME: ....
COULD BE DESCRIBED AS: ....
REMINDS ME OF (PERSON/CHARACTER):

WE ARE MOST ALIKE IN THESE WAYS:
....

WE ARE DIFFERENT IN THESE WAYS:
....

MY FAVORITE THING ABOUT THEM:
....

SISTER / BROTHER / IN-LAW

NAME: ....
COULD BE DESCRIBED AS: ....
REMINDS ME OF (PERSON / CHARACTER):
....

WE ARE MOST ALIKE IN THESE WAYS:
....

WE ARE DIFFERENT IN THESE WAYS:
....

MY FAVORITE THING ABOUT THEM:
....

SISTER / BROTHER / IN-LAW

NAME: ....
COULD BE DESCRIBED AS: ....
REMINDS ME OF (PERSON / CHARACTER):
....

WE ARE MOST ALIKE IN THESE WAYS:
....

WE ARE DIFFERENT IN THESE WAYS:
....

MY FAVORITE THING ABOUT THEM:
....

SISTER / BROTHER / IN-LAW

MY RELATIONSHIP WITH MY SIBLING(S): ....

MY SIBLING(S) TAUGHT ME: ....

51

CHOSEN FAMILY

THESE PEOPLE MIGHT AS WELL BE FAMILY:

NAME: ....

ROLE: ....

COULD BE DESCRIBED AS: ....

REMINDS ME OF THIS PERSON / CHARACTER:

WE ARE MOST ALIKE IN THESE WAYS:

....

....

WE ARE DIFFERENT IN THESE WAYS:

....

....

MY FAVORITE THING ABOUT THEM: ....

NAME: ....

ROLE: ....

COULD BE DESCRIBED AS: ....

REMINDS ME OF THIS PERSON / CHARACTER

WE ARE MOST ALIKE IN THESE WAYS:

....

WE ARE DIFFERENT IN THESE WAYS:

....

....

MY FAVORITE THING ABOUT THEM: ....

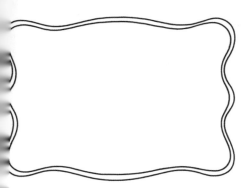

NAME: ....
ROLE: ....
THE BEST WAY TO DESCRIBE THEM:

MY FAVORITE THING ABOUT THEM:
....
....

NAME: ....
ROLE: ....
THE BEST WAY TO DESCRIBE THEM:

MY FAVORITE THING ABOUT THEM:
....
....

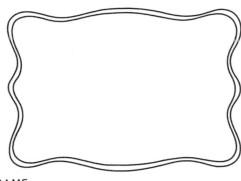

NAME: ....
ROLE: ....
THE BEST WAY TO DESCRIBE THEM:

MY FAVORITE THING ABOUT THEM:
....
....

NAME: ....
ROLE: ....
THE BEST WAY TO DESCRIBE THEM:

MY FAVORITE THING ABOUT THEM:
....
....

my realm

MY EPIC JOURNEY MAY TAKE ME MANY PLACES, BUT IT ALL STARTED HERE. THIS
THE REALM TO WHICH I BELONG, AND THE PLACES MOST IMPORTANT TO ME AND MY STO

MY LAIR

THIS IS MY HOMEBASE; THE PLACE I SLEEP AND CALL MY OWN.

LOCATION (CITY, COUNTRY, PLANE OF EXISTENCE, ETC):..

LEVEL OF SECRECY: OPEN TO PUBLIC ▭▭▭▭▭▭▭▭▭▭▭▭ TOP SECRET

OTHER RESIDENTS/GUESTS: ....

MY CURRENT HIDEOUT IS:
- ☐ HOUSE
- ☐ TRAILER
- ☐ HOBBIT HOLE
- ☐ MOUNTAIN (INCLUDES VOLCANO LAIRS)
- ☐ CASTLE
- ☐ AIRPLANE/SPACECRAFT
- ☐ CHURCH
- ☐ FOREST
- ☐ BARRACKS
- ☐ IN THE ENEMY CAMP

- ☐ APARTMENT
- ☐ SKYSCRAPER
- ☐ CAR
- ☐ BLUE PHONE BOOTH
- ☐ BOAT/SUBMARINE
- ☐ HOTEL
- ☐ MANSION
- ☐ CEMETERY
- ☐ LIVING HOST
- ☐ OTHER ....

MY HOME IS:
- ☐ COMFY
- ☐ DANGEROUS
- ☐ HEAVILY DECORATED
- ☐ CLEAN
- ☐ ABOVE GROUND
- ☐ FULL OF WEAPONS
- ☐ HAUNTED
- ☐ IN ANOTHER DIMENSION
- ☐ AUTOMATED BY ARTIFICIAL INTELLIGENCE

- ☐ SIMPLE
- ☐ GUARDED
- ☐ UTILITARIAN
- ☐ DISORGANIZED
- ☐ UNDERGROUND
- ☐ PROTECTED BY MAGIC
- ☐ IN A TREE
- ☐ IN THE AFTERLIFE
- ☐ OTHER ....

PROS OF LIVING HERE:

....
....
....
....
....
....
....
....
....

CONS OF LIVING HERE:

....
....
....
....
....
....
....
....
....

# PAST LAIRS

SOME STAY IN ONE PLACE ALL THEIR LIVES. OTHERS KEEP MOVING. AS FOR ME, THE NUMBER OF LAIRS I'VE INHABITED IS................ THEY ARE:

SHORTEST LENGTH OF RESIDENCE:...

LONGEST LENGTH OF RESIDENCE:..

REASONS FOR LEAVING:

☐ MOVED ON
☐ UNAFFORDABLE
☐ ADVENTURE WAS CALLING
☐ REALITY BECAME UNSTABLE
☐ I WAS CHOSEN AS TRIBUTE
☐ LOSS OF OXYGEN
☐ OTHER ....

☐ BREAK UP
☐ OUTGREW THE SPACE
☐ HAUNTED
☐ INFESTATION
☐ MY LIFE WAS AN ILLUSION
☐ INVASION

WHAT I REMEMBER MOST ABOUT EACH PLACE:

....
....
....
....
....

PROS OF LIVING THERE:

....
....
....
....
....

CONS OF LIVING THERE:

....
....
....
....
....

KNOWN HANGOUTS

BE IT OTHER TIME PERIODS, PLANETS, OR JUST THE LOCAL BOOKSTORE... THESE ARE MY HOMES AWAY FROM HOME.

WHEN I NEED TO RECHARGE, I GO TO: ....

I FEEL MOST AT HOME WHEN I: ....

WHEN I NEED TO BE ALONE, I LIKE TO: ....

DON'T BOTHER ME WHEN I'M: ....

WHEN I'M THERE, I LIKE TO: ....

WHILE I'M THERE, I'M OFTEN SEEN WITH:

WHEN I'M THERE, I LIKE TO: ....

WHILE I'M THERE, I'M OFTEN SEEN WITH:

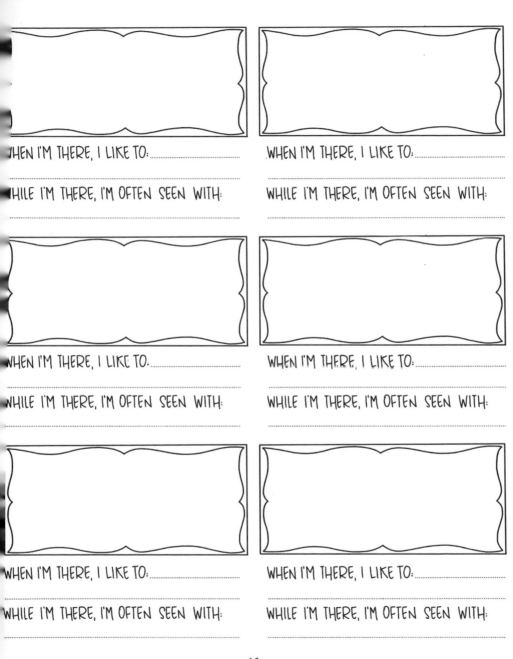

WHEN I'M THERE, I LIKE TO: ....

WHILE I'M THERE, I'M OFTEN SEEN WITH:

WHEN I'M THERE, I LIKE TO: ....

WHILE I'M THERE, I'M OFTEN SEEN WITH:

WHEN I'M THERE, I LIKE TO: ....

WHILE I'M THERE, I'M OFTEN SEEN WITH:

WHEN I'M THERE, I LIKE TO: ....

WHILE I'M THERE, I'M OFTEN SEEN WITH:

WHEN I'M THERE, I LIKE TO: ....

WHILE I'M THERE, I'M OFTEN SEEN WITH:

WHEN I'M THERE, I LIKE TO: ....

WHILE I'M THERE, I'M OFTEN SEEN WITH:

Dream Lair

GIVEN INFINITE FUNDS - OR SIGNIFICATE SCIENTIFIC ADVANCEMENTS -
I IMAGINE THE ULTIMATE LAIR TO LOOK SOMETHING LIKE THIS:

CATION: .... --

ZE: ....

FINING CHARACTERISTICS: ....

....

E BEST ROOM OR A FAVORITE FEATURE WITHIN THE LAIR:

WILL BE MINE WHEN:

- [ ] I'VE RETIRED
- [ ] I BECOME WHO I WANT TO BE
- [ ] THE TIME IS RIGHT
- [ ] I FIND MY TRUE LOVE
- [ ] THE WORLD IS PUT RIGHT
- [ ] WE HAVE THE TECHNOLOGY
- [ ] SCIENTIFIC ADVANCEMENTS OCCUR

- [ ] I CAN AFFORD IT
- [ ] I'VE FINISHED MY JOB
- [ ] MY QUEST IS COMPLETE
- [ ] EVERYONE FORGETS ABOUT ME
- [ ] THE WORLD ENDS
- [ ] DRAGONS ONCE AGAIN ROAM THE LAND
- [ ] OTHER ....

ORIGIN Story

EVERY GREAT ADVENTURE STARTS SOMEWHERE. EVERY HERO HAS HELP ALONG THE WAY. THIS IS THE PATH OF MY SELF-DISCOVERY, AND THOSE WHO AIDED ME IN IT.

DISCOVERING MY POWERS

WE DON'T ALL SUDDENLY BURST INTO FLAMES OR GAIN A TALKING CAT WHEN WE DISCOVER OUR POWER. THIS IS HOW I DISCOVERED MINE.

MY BEST TALENT:..

MY BEST SKILL:...

WHEN I DISCOVERED MY TALENT, I FELT:

☐ EXCITED

☐ ANGRY

☐ COMPLETE

☐ UNCERTAIN

☐ SCARED

☐ CONFUSED

☐ ANXIOUS

☐ OTHER ....

PEOPLE SEEM MOST AMAZED THAT I CAN:...

I'VE ALWAYS WANTED TO:...

MY MOST POWERFUL BODY PART:...

A TALENT FEW PEOPLE KNOW ABOUT:...

A MUNDANE SKILL I'M PROUD OF:...

MY PASSION IS:...

...IT RELIES [HEAVILY/VERY LITTLE] ON MY TALENT.

MY POWER MANIFESTS ITSELF AS:..

I WANT [EVERYONE/SOME PEOPLE/NO ONE] TO KNOW ABOUT MY POWER.

I WANT TO USE MY POWER FOR:

☐ GOOD

☐ JUSTICE

☐ POWER

☐ FAME

☐ EVIL

☐ MONETARY GAIN

☐ PROTECTION

☐ OTHER ....

SOMETIMES I WORRY MY POWER COULD LEAD TO:...

....

....

IF I LOST CONTROL OF MY POWERS:...

....

I IMMUNE TO:
[ ] FIRE
[ ] SLEEP
[ ] COLD
[ ] MAGIC
[ ] LOVE

[ ] WATER
[ ] HUNGER
[ ] HEAT
[ ] BOREDOM
[ ] OTHER ....

CONSIDER .... TO BE A SKILL INSIDE MY COMFORT ZONE.
.... IS A SKILL OUTSIDE MY COMFORT ZONE.

..I [WOULD/WOULD NOT] LIKE TO CHANGE THAT.

COULD... FOR SEVERAL HOURS STRAIGHT.

AM ABLE TO DO/PICK UP ON .... QUICKLY.

HOW I LOOK WHEN USING MY POWER:

A LIST OF MY GOOD HABITS:

DISCOVERING MY WEAKNESSES

MY MAIN WEAKNESS IS:...
I DISCOVERED THIS WEAKNESS:..

ACCEPTING MY WEAKNESS HAS BEEN:
☐ EASY   ☐ DIFFICULT
☐ IMPORTANT   ☐ INFURIATING
☐ RELIEVING   ☐ OTHER...............................

MY FOES HAVE USED MY WEAKNESS TO:..
THREE THINGS I CONSIDER TO BE MY PERSONALITY PITFALLS:..

....

....

A SUBJECT I STRUGGLE(D) WITH:..
MY SOCIAL ANXIETIES:..

....

IF I HAD TO FACE..I WOULD LOSE
....MAKES ME FREEZE UP
I'M TERRIFIED OF:...
...BECAUSE:...
I AM AFRAID OF..BUT CAN ENDURE IT IF NECESSARY
I HAVE TROUBLE DOING:...
I NEED HELP WITH:...
A FOOD I CAN'T RESIST:..
I CAN'T STOP MYSELF FROM BUYING:..
IN MY NIGHTMARES, I:..

....

70

HAVE A SOFT SPOT FOR:

POWERLESS AGAINST:
- ☐ FIRE
- ☐ SLEEP
- ☐ COLD
- ☐ MOST WEAPONS
- ☐ MAGIC
- ☐ CUTE ANIMALS

- ☐ WATER
- ☐ HUNGER
- ☐ HEAT
- ☐ BOREDOM
- ☐ LOVE
- ☐ OTHER ....

WHEN MY WEAKNESS IS USED AGAINST ME, I:
- ☐ SHUT OFF
- ☐ BECOME PARALYZED
- ☐ TURN EVIL
- ☐ FORGET WHO I AM
- ☐ OTHER ....

- ☐ BREAK DOWN EMOTIONALLY
- ☐ BECOME UNCONTROLLABLY ANGRY
- ☐ DISSOLVE INTO DUST
- ☐ MUST GRANT WISHES

POTENTIAL WAYS TO TURN MY WEAKNESS INTO A STRENGTH:

....

....

....

DISTRACTIONS: ....

....

....

....

....

A LIST OF MY BAD HABITS:

....

....

....

....

....

AN EMBARASSING TRUTH: ....

....

....

....

....

....

....

MENTORS

SKILLS AND DISCIPLINE ARE PASSED DOWN FROM TEACHER
TO STUDENT. THESE ARE MY TEACHERS.

MY PERSONAL MENTOR: ....

MY MENTOR TRAINED ME IN THE WAYS OF: ....

....

I ADMIRE MY MENTOR BECAUSE: ....

....

....

I COULD BE MORE LIKE MY MENTOR IF I: ....

....

SOMETHING MY MENTOR DOES WELL: ....

SOMETHING MY MENTOR TAUGHT ME: ....

....

SOMEONE FAMOUS I LOOK UP TO:...............

...BECAUSE:...............

I COULD BE MORE LIKE............IF I:...............

SOMETHING.......DOES WELL:...............
SOMETHING.........TAUGHT ME:...............

....

SOMEONE FAMOUS I LOOK UP TO:...............

...BECAUSE:...............

I COULD BE MORE LIKE............IF I:...............

SOMETHING.......DOES WELL:...............
SOMETHING.........TAUGHT ME:...............

....

SOMEONE IN MY FIELD OF WORK/STUDY
THAT I LOOK UP TO:...............
...BECAUSE:...............

I COULD BE MORE LIKE............IF I:...............

SOMETHING.......DOES WELL:...............

SOMETHING.........TAUGHT ME:...............

....

TRAINING

GREATNESS IS NOT GENETIC. IT IS LEARNED AND EARNED. THIS IS HOW.

I RECEIVED MY TRAINING IN A:
- ☐ SCHOOL
- ☐ MILITARY BASE
- ☐ TEMPLE
- ☐ APPRENTICESHIP
- ☐ SECRET SOCIETY
- ☐ THINK TANK
- ☐ ONE ON ONE WITH MY MENTOR
- ☐ IN THE MIDST OF BATTLE
- ☐ OTHER ....

IT TOOK ME ....TO REACH MY SKILL LEVEL.

THE HARDEST THING FOR ME TO LEARN WAS:...

NEW SKILLS LEARNED:...

OLD SKILLS HONED:...

PHYSICAL TRAINING:...

MENTAL TRAINING:...

EMOTIONAL TRAINING:...

TACTICAL TRAINING:...

my training montage

ACHIEVEMENTS

FIRST PARTY:

FIRST JOB:

FIRST BOSS:

FIRST TIME I GOT PAID FOR MY WORK:

FIRST BAND/MUSICIAN I BECAME OBSESSED WITH:

FIRST SONG I BECAME OBSESSED WITH:

FIRST SPORT I PLAYED:

FIRST SPORT I LOVED:

FIRST CELEBRITY CRUSH:

FIRST FICTIONAL CRUSH:

FIRST FICTIONAL CHARACTER I HATED:

FIRST BOOK I LOVED:

FIRST BOOK THAT MADE ME CRY:

FIRST BOOK I HATED:

FIRST MOVIE I LOVED:

FIRST MOVIE I COULDN'T STOP QUOTING:

FIRST FICTIONAL WORLD I WANTED TO LIVE IN:

FIRST VICE/ADDICTION:

FIRST FIGHT:

FIRST VEHICLE:

FIRST FOOD I DISCOVERED ON MY OWN:

FIRST FANDOM:

FIRST SCARY MOMENT:

FIRST MEMORABLE INJURY/ACCIDENT:

UNLOCKED

WE CAN'T HAVE EXPERIENCES WITHOUT A FIRST EXPERIENCE. THESE ARE MY FIRSTS.

FIRST TIME I TRAVELLED ALONE:...

FIRST EMERGENCY I HANDLED ON MY OWN:...

FIRST LONG TRIP:...

FIRST FOREIGN/FAR OFF PLACE I VISITED:...

FIRST HARD LIFE LESSON:...

FIRST BOOK I PUSHED ON OTHER PEOPLE:..

FIRST TV SHOW I LOVED:..

FIRST TV SHOW I PUSHED ON OTHER PEOPLE:...

FIRST TEACHER I LOVED:..

FIRST TEACHER I HATED:..

FIRST TIME I PAID MY OWN WAY:..

FIRST TIME I COULDN'T AFFORD WHAT I NEEDED:..

FIRST PERFECT DAY I CAN REMEMBER:..

FIRST TRULY TERRIBLE DAY I CAN REMEMBER:..

FIRST TIME I STOOD OUT:..

FIRST THING I WON:..

FIRST CONCERT I ATTENDED:..

FIRST OBSTACLE I OVERCAME:...

FIRST VACATION I REMEMBER:..

FIRST FRIEND I MADE THAT I'VE NEVER MET:...

FIRST VIDEO/COMPUTER GAME I LOVED:...

FIRST TIME I STEPPED OUT OF MY COMFORT ZONE:...

FIRST PET:...

FIRST OBSESSION:...

LEVELED UP

ACHIEVEMENTS BEYOND MY FIRSTS

THE Quest

THE TIME HAS COME TO SEE HOW I HAVE TAKEN EVERYTHING I HAVE LEARNED AND THE BUILDING BLOCKS OF WHO I AM, AND PUT THEM TO USE IN BECOMING WHO I AM TODAY.

A PORTRAIT OF ME AT THE START OF MY QUEST

Striking Out Alone

WHEN I FIRST LEFT HOME, I WAS:
- ☐ GOING TO SCHOOL
- ☐ GOING TO CAMP
- ☐ TRAVELLING WITH FRIENDS
- ☐ LOOKING FOR A JOB
- ☐ CHASED OUT
- ☐ ACTIVATED IN A LAB
- ☐ CALLED ON TO DEFEAT EVIL
- ☐ SEARCHING FOR A CURE/ANTIDOTE
- ☐ SUMMONED
- ☐ TRICKED BY A WIZARD
- ☐ JOINING A REVOLUTION
- ☐ OTHER:..................

I FELT:
- ☐ STRANGE
- ☐ SAD
- ☐ EXCITED
- ☐ HAPPY
- ☐ LOST
- ☐ OTHER:..................
- ☐ OVERWHELMED

MY FIRST REAL ADVENTURE WAS:...

...I WAS............YEARS OLD.

THROUGH THIS, I REALIZED I WAS GREAT AT:...........................

I ALSO REALIZED I WAS TERRIBLE AT:....................................

THAT FIRST ADVENTURE WAS:
- ☐ STRANGE
- ☐ EXCITING
- ☐ SCARY
- ☐ CHARMING
- ☐ ROMANTIC
- ☐ ENCHANTING
- ☐ EDUCATIONAL
- ☐ SILLY
- ☐ DARK
- ☐ OTHER:..................

WITHOUT A MENTOR/GUARDIAN TO SHOW ME THE WAY, I FOUND:...........

....

...I STRUGGLED TO:..

...BUT IT WASN'T LONG BEFORE:..

THE FIRST PERSON WHO SHOWED ME KINDNESS AFTER LEAVING HOME WAS:.......

THEY MADE ME REALIZE THAT:...

ALLIES

NOT EVERYONE CAN GAIN SECONDARY CHARACTER STATUS IN MY LIFE. THESE ARE THE ONES WHO AT LEAST GET THEIR NAME IN THE CREDITS:

COWORKERS / CLASSMATES / TEAMMATES...

...I CONSIDER COOLHEADED IN A CRISIS: ....

...I WOULD TELL SECRETS TO: ....

...I WOULD CHOOSE TO GO ON A QUEST WITH: ....

...I WOULD LIKE TO KNOW BETTER: ....

...I WOULD TEAM UP WITH ON A GHOST HUNT: ....

...I GRAVITATE TOWARD: ....

...WHEN IN DOUBT, WOULD GO TO THE LIBRARY: ....

...I LIKE, BUT DON'T NECESSARILY TRUST: ....

TOP ALLIES

NAME: ....

REASON FOR TOP 3 STATUS: ....

NAME: ....

REASON FOR TOP 3 STATUS: ....

NAME: ....

REASON FOR TOP 3 STATUS: ....

Allegiances

BE IT A GUILD, AN ARMY, A SECRET SOCIETY, OR A FELLOWSHIP, WE FIND OURSELVES IN GROUPS OF LIKE-MINDED PEOPLE. HERE ARE MY VARIOUS ALLEGIANCES.

GROUP:

AFFILIATION:

MY TITLE:

JOINED:

WITHOUT ME:

SIGIL:

GROUP:

AFFILIATION:

MY TITLE:

JOINED:

WITHOUT ME:

SIGIL:

GROUP:

AFFILIATION:

MY TITLE:

JOINED:

WITHOUT ME:

SIGIL:

GROUP:

AFFILIATION:

MY TITLE:

JOINED:

WITHOUT ME:

SIGIL:

GROUP:

AFFILIATION:

MY TITLE:

JOINED:

WITHOUT ME:

SIGIL:

THE GROUP MOST LIKELY TO RALLY BEHIND ME:

THE TWO GROUPS THAT WOULD NOT GET ALONG EASILY TOGETHER:

MEETS MOST FREQUENTLY:

MEETS LEAST FREQUENTLY:

ANIMAL COMPANIONS

NOT ALL OUR FRIENDS ARE THE SAME SPECIES AS WE ARE. PAST OR PRESENT, HERE ARE MINE.

NAME:..
SPECIES:..
DEFINING PHYSICAL TRAITS:........................
....
WHY THEY'RE SPECIAL:...............................
....

NAME:..
SPECIES:..
DEFINING PHYSICAL TRAITS:........................
....
WHY THEY'RE SPECIAL:...............................
....

NAME:..
SPECIES:..
DEFINING PHYSICAL TRAITS:
....
WHY THEY'RE SPECIAL:...............................
....

NAME:..
SPECIES:..
DEFINING PHYSICAL TRAITS:
....
WHY THEY'RE SPECIAL:...............................
....

NAME:..
SPECIES:..
DEFINING PHYSICAL TRAITS:
....
WHY THEY'RE SPECIAL:...............................
....

NAME:...
SPECIES:..
DEFINING PHYSICAL TRAITS:..............
....
WHY THEY'RE SPECIAL:......................
....

NAME:...
SPECIES:..
DEFINING PHYSICAL TRAITS:..............
....
WHY THEY'RE SPECIAL:......................
....

NAME:...
SPECIES:..
DEFINING PHYSICAL TRAITS:
....
WHY THEY'RE SPECIAL:......................
....
....

NAME:...
SPECIES:..
DEFINING PHYSICAL TRAITS:
....
WHY THEY'RE SPECIAL:......................
....
....

NAME:...
SPECIES:..
DEFINING PHYSICAL TRAITS:
....
WHY THEY'RE SPECIAL:......................
....
....

FRIENDS

NO ONE SHOULD HAVE TO WALK THEIR PATH ALONE. EVEN IF THEY CAN'T CARRY THE BURDEN OF MY QUEST FOR ME, THESE ARE THE ONES WILLING TO CARRY ME.

NAME:..
LAST KNOWN LOCATION:......................................
FRIENDSHIP ESTABLISHED:...................................
FIRST MET:..
FRIENDSHIP BUILT ON THE FOUNDATION OF:

....
I WOULD DESCRIBE THEM AS:.................................
....

NAME:..
LAST KNOWN LOCATION:......................................
FRIENDSHIP ESTABLISHED:...................................
FIRST MET:..
FRIENDSHIP BUILT ON THE FOUNDATION OF:

....
I WOULD DESCRIBE THEM AS:.................................
....

NAME:..
LAST KNOWN LOCATION:......................................
FRIENDSHIP ESTABLISHED:...................................
FIRST MET:..
FRIENDSHIP BUILT ON THE FOUNDATION OF:

....
I WOULD DESCRIBE THEM AS:.................................
....

90

NAME:

LAST KNOWN LOCATION:

FRIENDSHIP ESTABLISHED:

FIRST MET:

FRIENDSHIP BUILT ON THE FOUNDATION OF:

I WOULD DESCRIBE THEM AS:

NAME:

LAST KNOWN LOCATION:

FRIENDSHIP ESTABLISHED:

FIRST MET:

FRIENDSHIP BUILT ON THE FOUNDATION OF:

I WOULD DESCRIBE THEM AS:

NAME:

LAST KNOWN LOCATION:

FRIENDSHIP ESTABLISHED:

FIRST MET:

FRIENDSHIP BUILT ON THE FOUNDATION OF:

I WOULD DESCRIBE THEM AS:

MY BEST FRIEND:

..WE FORGED AN UNBREAKABLE BOND THROUGH:

THE FRIEND I AM MOST SIMILAR TO:...
THE FRIEND MOST PEOPLE WOULD BE SURPRISED I HAVE:...
THE FRIEND I HAVE KNOWN THE LONGEST:...
MY MOST RECENT FRIEND:...
I WOULD MAKE AN UNBREAKABLE VOW FOR:..
I LIVE CLOSEST TO:...
I WOULD ENTRUST................................TO CARRY ON WITH MY QUEST IN MY ABSENCE.
....WOULD BE BY MY SIDE DURING MY TRAINING MONTAG
MY DAILY-LIFE SIDEKICK:..
I CAN COUNT ON.......................TO FIND ME AT MY FAVORITE HIDEOUT.
WHEN THERE'S DRAMA, THERE'S:...
AN UNEXPECTED FRIEND:...
MY WILDEST FRIEND:...

IF I HAD TO CHOOSE ONE FRIEND FOR EACH OF THESE ADVENTURES, I WOULD PICK:
....TO BE BY MY SIDE IN BATTLE.
....TO HELP ME WHEN I'M IN PAIN.
....TO KNOCK SENSE INTO ME.
....TO DEFEND ME.
....TO THROW ME A PARTY.
....TO TESTIFY FOR ME.
....TO AVENGE MY DEATH.

FIVE THINGS THAT MAKE A FRIEND INTO A BEST FRIEND:...
....
....

FRIENDS I'VE LOST TOUCH WITH:...

FRIENDS WHO NOW RESIDE IN THE ENEMY CAMP:...
REASON:..

SHIPS

THESE ARE THE RELATIONSHIPS, PAST, PRESENT, AND POTENTIAL, IN MY LIFE THUS FAR.
THIS IS WHERE THE ROMANCE IS. OR ISN'T.

WHAT I FIND ATTRACTIVE: ....

WHAT I FIND UNATTRACTIVE: ....

First Loves

MY FIRST CRUSH:

NAME: .... AGE: ....
[WAS/WAS NOT] AWARE OF MY FEELINGS.

LOOKING BACK, I WONDER: ....

THIS CRUSH WAS:
- ☐ SOMETHING I GOT OVER
- ☐ THE ONE THAT GOT AWAY
- ☐ THE GREATEST LOVE OF MY LIFE
- ☐ OTHER: ....

- ☐ EASILY FORGOTTEN
- ☐ AN OBSESSION
- ☐ THE RESULT OF MAGIC/TRICKERY

MY FIRST KISS: ....
...IT:
- ☐ LED TO MORE
- ☐ ENDED ALL HOPES OF ROMANCE
- ☐ OTHER: ....

- ☐ WAS NOT MEMORABLE
- ☐ WAS HARD TO TOP

THE ALLURE OF FIRST LOVE: ....
IT WASN'T UNTIL I MET .... THAT I REALLY KNEW WHAT LOVE WAS.
LOVE MAKES ME FEEL: ....

SUNKEN

THE SHIPS THAT SAILED, BUT MET UNTIMELY ENDS.

NAME:...
DURATION:...
THINGS I LIKED ABOUT THEM:...............
....
....

THINGS I DISLIKED ABOUT THEM:..........
....

REASON(S) FOR ENDING:........................
....

HOW I FELT THEN:..
HOW I FEEL NOW:.......................................

NAME:...
DURATION:...
THINGS I LIKED ABOUT THEM:...............
....

THINGS I DISLIKED ABOUT THEM:..........
....

REASON(S) FOR ENDING:........................
....

HOW I FELT THEN:..
HOW I FEEL NOW:.......................................

NAME:...
DURATION:...
THINGS I LIKED ABOUT THEM:...............
....
....

THINGS I DISLIKED ABOUT THEM:..........
....

REASON(S) FOR ENDING:........................
....

HOW I FELT THEN:..
HOW I FEEL NOW:.......................................

NAME:...
DURATION:...
THINGS I LIKED ABOUT THEM:...............
....

THINGS I DISLIKED ABOUT THEM:..........
....

REASON(S) FOR ENDING:........................
....

HOW I FELT THEN:..
HOW I FEEL NOW:.......................................

STUCK IN HARBOR

SHIPS THAT WILL PROBABLY NEVER SAIL UNLESS MAGIC IS INVOLVED.

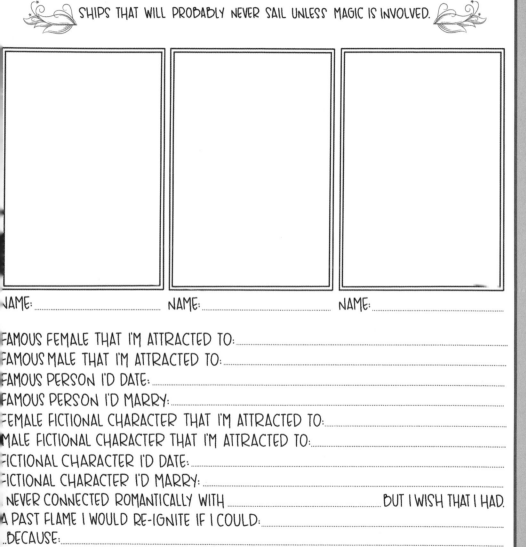

NAME: .... NAME: .... NAME: ....

FAMOUS FEMALE THAT I'M ATTRACTED TO: ....

FAMOUS MALE THAT I'M ATTRACTED TO: ....

FAMOUS PERSON I'D DATE: ....

FAMOUS PERSON I'D MARRY: ....

FEMALE FICTIONAL CHARACTER THAT I'M ATTRACTED TO: ....

MALE FICTIONAL CHARACTER THAT I'M ATTRACTED TO: ....

FICTIONAL CHARACTER I'D DATE: ....

FICTIONAL CHARACTER I'D MARRY: ....

I NEVER CONNECTED ROMANTICALLY WITH .... BUT I WISH THAT I HAD.

A PAST FLAME I WOULD RE-IGNITE IF I COULD: ....

...BECAUSE: ....

95

Sailing

THIS IS THE RELATIONSHIP THAT IS HAPPENING NOW, SAILING THROUGH SMOOTH AND ROUGH SEAS:

CURRENTLY IN A RELATIONSHIP WITH: ....
WE HAVE KNOWN EACH OTHER SINCE: ....
WE HAVE BEEN TOGETHER FOR: ....
WE MET: ....
MY FAVORITE THINGS ABOUT THEM: ....
....

THINGS I WOULDN'T MIND CHANGING ABOUT THEM: ....
....

A FAMOUS PERSON THEY SEEM MOST LIKE: ....
A FICTIONAL CHARACTER THEY ARE MOST LIKE: ....
WE ARE MOST ALIKE IN THESE WAYS: ....
....

WE ARE LEAST ALIKE IN THESE WAYS: ....
....

A SPECIAL MEMORY OF THEM: ....

SOMETHING THEY ALWAYS SAY: ....

THREE WORDS TO DESCRIBE THEM: ....
THREE WORDS THEY'D USE TO DESCRIBE THEMSELVES: ....
SOMETHING THEY KNOW ABOUT ME THAT FEW, IF ANY, DO: ....
....

SOMETHING I KNOW ABOUT THEM THAT FEW, IF ANY, DO: ....
....

THEIR CHARACTER CLASS: ....
OUR FAVORITE THING TO DO TOGETHER: ....
....

RIVALS

NOT ALL ANTAGONISTS ARE EVIL OR MY ENEMIES. SOME OF THEM JUST HAPPEN TO NOT BE MY FRIENDS.

SOMEONE I CONSIDER UNRELIABLE:

SOMEONE I DISTRUST:

SOMEONE I CONSIDER TO BE FAKE:

SOMEONE I DISAGREE WITH OFTEN:

MOST ANNOYING PERSON I KNOW:

...THEY ANNOY ME BECAUSE:

I AM FRIENDS WITH THIS PERSON ONLY BECAUSE IT'S POLITE TO BE:

I AM COMPETITIVE WITH:

IT IS [FRIENDLY / UNFRIENDLY] COMPETITION

OTHER RIVALS I'VE ENCOUNTERED:

pet peeves

A LIST OF THINGS THAT ANTAGONIZE ME

VILLAINS

I CONSIDER THIS PERSON MY ENEMY: ....

...WE BECAME ENEMIES WHEN: ....

...IT WAS .... FAULT.

...[I WAS / THEY WERE]...

☐ LIED TO
☐ BETRAYED
☐ ATTACKED
☐ BULLIED
☐ INSULTED

☐ THROWN UNDER THE BUS
☐ PROVOKED
☐ HURT
☐ SLANDERED
☐ OTHER: ....

...BY [THEM / ME].

HOW I FELT WHEN WE BECAME ENEMIES: ....

....

HOW I FEEL ABOUT THEM NOW: ....

....

[I / THEY]...

☐ HAVE
☐ AM / ARE WORKING
☐ WILL
☐ AM / ARE CONSIDERING
☐ WILL NEVER

...FORGIVE(N) [THEM / ME].

[I / THEY]...

☐ HAVE
☐ AM / ARE WORKING
☐ WILL
☐ AM / ARE CONSIDERING
☐ WILL NEVER

...FORGET [THEM / ME].

MY ENEMY AND I LOCKED IN
glorious battle

MONSTERS

THESE ARE THE BEASTS THAT CAUSE STRUGGLES IN MY LIFE BE IT HUMAN, CREATURE OR CONDITION. I WILL CROSS THEM OFF AS I VANQUISH THEM.

☐ vanquished
THE FEARSOME: ....
...SO CALLED BECAUSE: ....
....

THE KEY TO VANQUISHING THIS MONSTER: ....
....

☐ vanquished
THE WICKED: ....
...SO CALLED BECAUSE: ....
....

THE KEY TO VANQUISHING THIS MONSTER: ....
....

☐ vanquished
THE TRICKSY: ....
...SO CALLED BECAUSE: ....
....

THE KEY TO VANQUISHING THIS MONSTER: ....
....

☐ vanquished
THE RUTHLESS: ....
...SO CALLED BECAUSE: ....
....

THE KEY TO VANQUISHING THIS MONSTER: ....
....
....

☐ vanquished

THE_____ :_____

...SO CALLED BECAUSE:_____

_____

THE KEY TO VANQUISHING THIS MONSTER:_____

_____

☐ vanquished

THE_____ :_____

...SO CALLED BECAUSE:_____

_____

THE KEY TO VANQUISHING THIS MONSTER:_____

_____

☐ vanquished

THE_____ :_____

...SO CALLED BECAUSE:_____

_____

THE KEY TO VANQUISHING THIS MONSTER:_____

_____

☐ vanquished

THE_____ :_____

...SO CALLED BECAUSE:_____

_____

THE KEY TO VANQUISHING THIS MONSTER:_____

_____

☐ vanquished

THE_____ :_____

...SO CALLED BECAUSE:_____

_____

THE KEY TO VANQUISHING THIS MONSTER:_____

_____

TRIALS ᴬᴺᴰ TRIBULATIONS

I SHOULD LOCK THIS SECTION UP AND THROW AWAY THE KEY, BUT THE MONSTERS AND VILLAINS, HAVING HAD A HAND - OR CLAW - IN THESE TRIALS THEMSELVES, ALREADY KNOW THE SCORE. ACCEPTING WHAT OTHERS COULD USE AGAINST ME MEANS I CAN USE IT AS ARMOR INSTEAD. SO HERE IS WHAT I HAVE BEEN THROUGH:

MY BIGGEST BATTLE WAS WITH:..

...I FOUGHT FOR:..

...MY FOE'S STRENGTHS WERE:..

...NEXT TIME, FACING THIS/A SIMILAR FOE, I WILL:..

...AFTER THE BATTLE, MY FOE AND I:

☐ NEVER SAW EACH OTHER AGAIN
☐ REMAINED MORTAL ENEMIES
☐ FOUGHT TIME AND TIME AGAIN
☐ JOINED FORCES
☐ FORGED A USEFUL TRUTH
☐ TEAMED UP TO DEFEAT A COMMON ENEMY
☐ BECAME FRIENDS
☐ HAD A WHIRLWIND ROMANCE
☐ FELL IN LOVE
☐ TOOK OVER THE WORLD
☐ OTHER:..

I HAVE BEEN FIRED FROM A JOB: Y/N
...THE CIRCUMSTANCES WERE:..
....

I HAVE BEEN REJECTED ON A DATE: Y/N
...THE CIRCUMSTANCES WERE:..
....

SOMETHING I AM ASHAMED OF:..
....

IN A CRISIS, MY RESPONSE TENDS TO BE: [FIGHT/FLIGHT/FREEZE].

THE WORST THING THAT HAS EVER HAPPENED TO ME: ....

....

   ...HOW I IMAGINED I WOULD REACT TO A SITUATION LIKE THAT: ....

....

   ...HOW I ACTUALLY REACTED: ....

....

   ...HOW I FELT: ....
   ...HOW I SURVIVED: ....

....

   ...I HAD HELP FROM: ....

THE BEST THING THAT HAS EVER HAPPENED TO ME: ....

....

   ...HOW I IMAGINED I WOULD REACT TO A SITUATION LIKE THAT: ....

....

   ...HOW I ACTUALLY REACTED: ....

....

   ...HOW I FELT: ....

....

   ...I HAD HELP FROM: ....

THE SCARIEST THING THAT HAS EVER HAPPENED TO ME: ....

....

   ...HOW I IMAGINED I WOULD REACT TO A SITUATION LIKE THAT: ....

....

   ...HOW I ACTUALLY REACTED: ....

....

   ...HOW I FELT: ....
   ...HOW I SURVIVED: ....

....

   ...I HAD HELP FROM: ....

THE Legend

NO EPIC ADVENTURE   EVER RUNS
SMOOTHLY—AND LIFE CERTAINLY DOESN'T PULL
ANY PUNCHES. I HAVE BEEN THROUGH MANY THINGS,
GOOD AND BAD. THESE ARE MY DEFINING MOMENTS,
MY ROUGH SEAS, AND THE LEGACY I'LL LEAVE BEHIND.

A PORTRAIT OF ME AT THE END OF MY QUEST

MOMENTS OF TRUTH

THESE ARE THE MOMENTS THAT CHANGED MY LIFE, GOOD OR BAD:

THE LOWEST MOMENT OF MY LIFE:

THE GREATEST MOMENT OF MY LIFE:

THE SCARIEST MOMENT OF MY LIFE:

THE SADDEST MOMENT OF MY LIFE:

MY MOST SHAMEFUL MOMENT:

THE PROUDEST MOMENT OF MY LIFE:

MY MOST EMBARASSING MOMENT: ....

....

....

MY FUNNIEST MOMENT: ....

....

....

THE HAPPIEST MOMENT OF MY LIFE: ....

....

....

THE MOMENT I FELT MOST ACCOMPLISHED: ....

....

....

THE MOMENT I FELT LEAST ACCOMPLISHED: ....

....

....

MY MOST TRIUMPHANT MOMENT: ....

....

....

MY BRAVEST MOMENT: ....

....

....

....

Saving the Day

THE BEST THING I'VE EVER DONE: ....

....

MY FIGHT SONG: ....

MY PERSONAL MANTRA: ....

THINGS I DO THAT HELP ME SUCCEED: ....

....

I AM MOST DRIVEN WHEN: ....

....

....

THINGS I HAVE DONE THAT HAVE IMPACTED/INFLUENCED OTHERS: .....

....

....

....

....

....

....

....

....

IF THE INNER ME MATCHED THE OUTER ME, I'D LOOK LIKE:

DEFEATS and REGRETS

Triumphs

TREASURES
lost and won

MY MOST PRIZED POSSESSION:

POSSESSIONS I WOULD HIDE A PIECE OF MY SOUL IN (IF I WAS INTO THAT SORT OF THING):

THINGS I HAVE LOST AND MISS:

THINGS I HAVE LOST BUT DON'T MISS:

PEOPLE I HAVE LOST AND MISS:

PEOPLE I HAVE LOST BUT DON'T MISS:

....IS MY PRECIOUS.

SOMEONE I CONSIDER A TREASURE:

MY...IS/ARE IRREPLACEABLE.

THINGS I COLLECT:

MOST EXCITING TREASURE I'VE FOUND:

THINGS I SEARCH FOR TO ADD TO MY HOARD:

Legacy

THIS IS HOW I WANT TO BE REMEMBERED AND WHO I MAY BE REMEMBERED BY.

I [HAVE / WANT] .... KIDS.
NAME(S) / POTENTIAL NAME(S):

....
....

THEY ARE / I HOPE THEY'D BE LIKE:

....
....
....

THIS IS HOW I WANT TO BE REMEMBERED BY FRIENDS AND FAMILY:

....
....
....
....
....

THIS IS HOW I WANT TO BE REMEMBERED IN MY WORK:

....
....
....
....
....

WHAT MY LEGACY
LOOKS LIKE TO ME

MORAL OF THE Story

I HAVE SURVIVED MY QUEST (THUS FAR) AND REACHED THE END OF THIS ACCOUNT OF MY LEGENDARY LIFE. FROM ALL I HAVE WRITTEN HERE, THE FOLLOWING PAGES ARE WHAT I HAVE LEARNED ABOUT MYSELF.

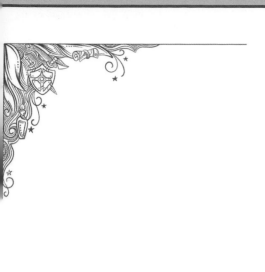

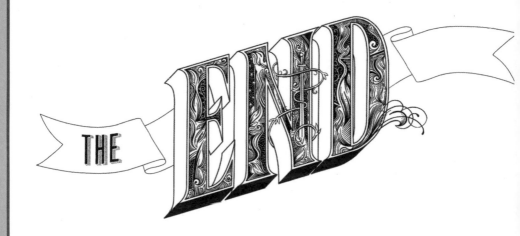

THE END